Mending Worlds

Stephen Spanoudis

Mending Worlds

Copyright © 2022 Stephen L. Spanoudis

Mending Worlds

DEDICATION

To the rest of the Chorus. You know who you are.

by Stephen Spanoudis

Novels:
Mettle
Explorers
Wanderers
Defender
Ethos
Ion
Scattered to the Winds
Final Orbit

Novellas and Other Stories:
The Ghost and the Volcano
To the Gates of the Western Sea
Tethered to the Sky

Poetry:
Voices, Context and Dreams
Mending Worlds

Serialized Adventures:

Roger and Phoebe (on Kindle Vella)
Third Citizen of Dreams (on Kindle Vella)

Contents

Preface

Having a regular schedule of in-person and video performances helped me finish my first poetry collection, and led me to accumulate material for a second one. Thanks to Kai, Nazeelah, Marnino, and others for giving me regular targets to hit.

There are many voices here, some created in response to chorus subjects, some in response to the world around me, and some as a result of the twists and turns that life inevitably takes. Sadly, we live in a time where, for many, the past few years have included war, fear, loss, and grief. Those subjects are all covered here. The book title is from an older poem I unearthed and appended as the final piece – written for *Scattered to the Winds* – Book VII of *The Republic of Dreams* series (marked *RoD*) – a volume that is, as of this writing, still unfinished. There are other voices here from *RoD*, intended to revisit things from a new perspective, or flesh-out characters that received only limited screen time in prose. When I perform them in public, I call them Animé pieces, because that is the genre they are closest to. However, be forewarned – they are not necessarily an exact match to the novels.

As I compiled this volume, I was also trying to finish *Roger and Phoebe (Done!)*, and make headway on *Scattered to the Winds*, on *Stars and Alligators*, and on *Third Citizen of Dreams*, and debating whether or not to start *Emissary*. I think I have learned that the best way to stay productive is simply to keep writing, and to keep observing the world around us. One flows into the other.

Steve Spanoudis, Coral Springs, Florida, November 2022

I.   In the North

⌘ The Islands Within

This house at night is islands of light
Separated by seas of darkness.
Each surmounted by the slender tree
Of a desk or table lamp casting
Hemispheres of illumination
Upon the surfaces where we live
And eat and breath and bathe and work
And nestle together beneath
Protective sheets against those things
That slither and skitter
And go bump in the night.

So many of the metaphors of our language
Deal with the battles of light and darkness,
Despite the very clear knowledge of Science
That Darkness is only a place where
Our feeble eyes cannot see the infrared
Or ultraviolet or cosmic rays that
Illuminate everything everywhere
On some level. It is like the sounds
That do not scare us because we,

Limited creatures that we are,
Cannot hear them or conceive
That they even exist. Too high
Or too low or too quiet.

But they are there, nevertheless,
The lights and the sounds,
Pervading the silence and the darkness,
Connecting us and everything else
Like gravity itself - the most invisible
Of all things, yet the most important
Of all forms of attraction.

And I will add one more thing,
An important thing, to that list
Of things that connects us islands
To each other: the thought of each other,
The human bonds of knowledge and
Affection and experience that bind
Us together in the darkness and the light.

These too are invisible, yet we know
Beyond a doubt that they are there.
I argue that the strings of the heart are
No more ephemeral than those strings
The physicists theorize about,
That are too small to see, but they insist
Make up all we see, and are,
And ever will be. So be it. I will define
My own islands within, connecting,
Vibrating, attracting, repelling,
The other living things within

Their own hemispheres of light
In this house tonight, and every night.

⌘ Unsilent Spring

For the People of Ukraine

Bombs bloom noisily,
Shattering the walled silence
Of apartment blocks
In lifeless cities, obliterated
By the megalomania
Of the lone lunatic left over
From the long-forgotten cold war
Of the last century,
While the west wails woefully
But can do little to help those
Beset by invaders inching
Ever closer to the doorways
Of forty-four million souls,
Whose only crime was to wish
To live their little lives in peace,
And to learn how to build their
New Old country into a place
Where their Children's
Children could find their own
Version of peace, and likewise,
Proudly pay it forward.

When all is said and done,
And the many dead are dead,

And millions more are forever displaced,
And homes and schools and hospitals
Are pulverized to dust,
Or burned to greasy gray ash,
As ignorant armies sent
From an ignorant homeland
Lash out at people who look
Just like their mothers and brothers,
Not knowing why they do so,
Just following orders.

The knowledge that that excuse,
That ignorance, that arrogance,
Did not disappear
With the last century
Is almost as sad
As the war itself,
As the new century
Re-lives all of the horrors
Of the old one
At hyperspeed.

And while there is no remedy,
Reluctant or otherwise, in sight
For the current suffering,
We can take some small solace
In the belief that somewhere,
Not too far down this road,
If the equation of this universe
Has any semblance
Of balance, that Karma will
Rear its head, and though

It cannot retrieve the dead,
As spring comes to the land
Of blue skies and sunflowers,
Maybe something will manage
To grow from the dust,
And the blood,
And the ashes,
And the tears.
Something scarred and stunted,
But surviving nonetheless.

⌘ The Things We Inherit

The things we inherit are not things,
I mean, yes of course there are things:
A household to be dealt with,
Personal possessions to be distributed,
Bills to pay. Thanks to be given.
The usual social debts and obligations.

But then there are the things that are not things,
The way of looking at the world,
The turns of phrase and favorite homilies,
The facial features from parent A and parent B,
The physical size, shape, and lifespan.

And then there are other not-thing things,
The tendencies and propensities,
The beliefs and attitudes,
The fears and flash points,

And hopefully, the coping skills
To help us deal with all of the above.

It bears reminding that we are not
The only shapers of this clay
That we wear upon our bones,
Or the only collector of the stones
That rattle about inside our skulls.
The refrigerator has little role
In choosing the cloud of magnetic mementos
That becomes its outer skin in youth,
And give color to its older age.

And we must remember that grief
Is a clouded lens, and near-sighted,
And that somewhere down this path
As we stumble onward through life
There will be, if not clarity, at least
A vision of sorts, and a distillation
Of these things our parents
Inherited from their parents,
And our children have inherited from us.

We have always been adept, as a family,
In dealing with the things that are things.
The rest we teach ourselves
Out of necessity. A sadly recurring
Necessity that builds a resilient
Muscle memory we do not want,
But inherit nonetheless.

And only after we have lost those

Who came before us, and
Some time and space have elapsed,
Does the clouded lens clear enough
So that we can begin finally
To understand the things
That shaped the trajectory
Of their lives, and in doing so, realize
What we must do to steer our own.

⌘ Novice (RoD)

Merope Lim, Master of
The School of Spinning Birds,
Addressed a slender teenage boy,
Younger sibling to one of her
Better students. This would usually
Be a simple dismissal. But this decision
Would prove to be far from simple.
"I teach advanced *T'ai chi ch'uan*.
Why should I waste my time
Instructing a novice?"

His reply was clear and
Confidently resolute:
"Because I will not be a novice
For long. I learn quickly.
What you tell me once,
I will remember always.
I am quick, agile, and unafraid.

I am respectful and hardworking.
I do not brag or complain.
If you tell me I must practice a thing
A thousand times, I will.
I finish what I start.
I make few promises,
But I keep them all."

The boy bowed deeply,
Bending his body until his face
Touched his knees, then standing
Crisply at attention.

"A good manifesto," she observed.
"Well planned, and well executed.
Now shed your outer clothing.
Let me see what there is to work with."
He stripped off his clothes and
Patiently awaited her inspection.

Startled, she walked in slow circles,
Observing, and then tracing her fingers
Over each of his scars. There were dozens.
He shivered at the lightness of her touch,
And the strange feel of her slender fingers
Moving across the ravaged areas of his skin.

"Your brother did not explain this.
You are not a novice. No one
Who has lived through all of *this*
Could possibly be called a novice."

She ran her fingertips over the
Evil eye charm he wore around his neck.
It prickled his skin in response to her touch.
"What is this?"
                    "A ward against Death."
"It works?"
                    "So far."
"Your name, in your native tongue,
It means what?"
                    "Defender."

She nodded slowly. "Appropriate.
I see no fear in you. I see honesty.
I see strength and resolve.
Yes, I have decided
That I will teach you.
Mondays and Wednesdays at 1600 hours.
Lessons last as long as required –
A minute, an hour, a day, a lifetime.
Understood?"
                    "Yes, Master."
Afterwards, she shuddered
At what the scars represented,
At the words of pain and suffering
The battles between Life and Death
Had written across the child's skin.
Such a long catalogue
For someone so very young.
Longer, even, than her own.

"Not a novice." She whispered.

⌘ Kingdom of Thistles

In the center of Emerald Green,
Somewhere between playgrounds
And ballfields and swingsets,
There is a hillside covered
In wildflowers, some common,
Some oddly mysterious
With unexpected colors and textures,
Forming intricately woven patterns
Too complex for our minds to
Unravel or appreciate, unless,
On a summer's evening,
We kneel beside it in the grass
And stare quietly for an hour
Or two or three, as birds and insects
Furtively come and go, and come and go,
And the wind ripples through the long
Slender grasses, and their ripples ripple through us,
And the slowly slanting summer sun
Slides toward its vanishing point,
It's hazy horizontal home,
Then, maybe then, if we are lucky,
Our minds will dissect and untangle
And unearth, on some paltry level
Of comprehension, the teeming complexity
Life can create, and evolve, and reveal,
And renew, year after year,
When left to its own designs.

But once we have gotten

Our groggy human minds around
That mystery, and brought ourselves
Back from the maze of worlds
Within worlds within worlds,
We might glance up and see, in its center,
Something entirely different:
A thicket so dense we cannot enter
Or even glimpse what lies inside.
A place where this year's green thistles
And last year's brown thistles
And thistles from prior years, faded to
A slender, pale, bone-like gray,
Rise three meters into the air
With interwoven acanthacine leaves
And thorn-armored crowns
To create an impenetrability
We cannot comprehend,
Guarding a secret we cannot
Imagine, and experience either
A sense of wonder, or of fear, for we
Simple creatures often fear what we
Cannot understand, or possess,
Or control. Wisdom, perhaps, is
To know that that that lives within,
Within this Kingdom of Thistles,
Is too thorny for us to deal with
And is something best left alone.

What wisdom really is, perhaps,
Perhaps, is the ability to accept
The existence of things we cannot
Know, and will not know, no matter

How long or how hard we seek for
An answer. Life, complex though it may be,
Simply is. There is no answer
Because the question itself
May be beyond us. Or worse yet,
What if there is no question?
Life does not need to be the answer to anything.
And neither, in point of fact, do we.

⌘ Eventually, After the Fire Burns

Grief is the hardest of all emotions
To put into words, not because
There are no words for it -
There are all too many -
But because it draws
A sharp, fiery, border of pain
Around those precious things
We want most to hold onto,
And it burns us each time
We reach into the past for memories
Of those who are no longer here,
Of those who shared in our lives,
And in our personal history,
Who were part of making us
Into the person that we are.

For some, catharsis comes in time,
Healing of a sort. But for many,
Maybe most, what passes for closure

Is a dark, ragged place where
That fiery edge has burned away
Our feelings. Scabbed them over.
Compartmentalized them, in ways
We can mostly deal with.

Time is an ally here, slowly
Building bridges for us
Across the fire-ravaged plain,
Mapping a new route for us
So that, if we cannot grasp
All that we want, hopefully,
In quiet moments of peace
And in desperate moments of fear,
We can find what we most need.

⌘ Occult

Occult is a misunderstood word.
It has not one meaning, but two.
The first means things unexplained,
To which we ascribe supernatural means,
And assign dark powers, evil intents,
And the utter certainty that, sooner or later,
Something wicked this way comes.

The other is a thing that is both more,
And less to be feared. It means, simply,
Things hidden from view, that have
No apparent cause, or symptom.

Astronomical objects are subject
To occultation. During an eclipse, the sun itself
Becomes a member of the occult,
Though only for the briefest of moments.

That is so rare and so disconcerting
It is no little wonder that
The two meanings are often conflated.
It also implies that there are no absolutes
In this universe, when light itself can,
If only for that brief interval,
Be coaxed to join the dark side.

But if that is so, it is also true,
That the journey through darkness
Is not infinitely long, and afterwards,
There is a return to the visible,
To color and contrast, to shadows and illumination.
Dawn breaks, or the storm passes, or a window opens,
And life has what it needs to continue.

Perhaps what it means for us
Is that we do not fully appreciate the stars
Who bathe us in their glow,
Who we take for granted,
Until they are absent.
Until their light is gone from us,
Until those who have illuminated our lives
Are forever hidden from view, often,
Seemingly, without cause, or reason.

But there are many people in this world.

If we lose those who are dear to us,
It is also true, or at least, statistically likely,
That somewhere, out there, is someone else
That could brighten your life, but they too
May be battling through a painful eclipse,
And searching, desperately, for a source of light.

⌘ Playmates

The winds are whipping their way
Around this old house's square corners,
And herding the autumn leaves
As they tumble down the street,
To find a final resting place
Before winter rains mold them
To the shape of their forever home,
And winter snows cover them
From the light, and the air, and the cold,
And press them against the soil
Until worms and microbes finish feasting
And they become one with the world.

Their salad days are long gone,
Not that oak and maple leaves,
Or beach or gum tree leaves ever
Made up any salad that I ever saw.

Yet they had their time in the sun,
Waxed lush and green, rippling
Their ribs in spring's warm welcome

And flushed fully green
In summer's sultry sunsets, preparing
For their big debut as golden
Fall foliage against brilliant blue sky.

And when the snows cover them,
And they begin the process
Of dissolving into nothingness,
Who will the winds have to play with?

⌘ The Ghosts of Sharon Wood

There are ghosts in these woods,
In the older part of the forest.
Do children venture near? Or do they
Fear what lingers among the leaves?

The ghosts are not human,
Nor are they entirely dead,
But are so long lived it is valid
To count them among the undead.

I sense their looming presence,
Especially when they are enveloped
In fall's canopy of golden hair
And rain blackens their trunks.

Their arms stretch so high above me
And spread so far outward
I cannot tell where one ends

And another's branches begin.

These oaks and maples are ancient,
Old-growth wood. Their truncated
Lower limbs look like stumps of
Severed arms, missing their hands

As they jut out at odd angles,
Impervious to the ages,
But bearing the scars of lightning,
And wind and rain and snow.

These Ghosts serve as host
To innumerable living things
That thrive in the dead or
Undead portions of the trees,

Lichens and fungi, mosses,
Owls, robins, squirrels, insects,
And millions of microbes
Smaller than the eye can see.

There are ghosts in these woods,
I revere their presence,
Wondering what wisdom
Their roots have revealed from
Mining minerals in the earth,

Or what hoarded history
Their round rings retain,
Charting the changing seasons
Century by slow century.

Or how many times their
Wind-stretched fingers
Have strived to reach
The first rays of sunrise,

Or the last glimmers of sunset,
Or how many more times
They will stand sentinel
Through dawns and dusks to come.

There are ghosts in these woods,
But not even they know,
Not even the wending wind knows,
The answer to that last question.

⌘ Warmth

My cousin visited today, bringing her adult children.
We ate a savory meal I fussed over all morning,
Filled with deep flavors, and colors and textures,
And aromas that will make the house
Feel happily lived-in for the entire day.

It was a rare visit, filled with smiles
And conversation, And I wanted to fill it
With colorful memories to last
Until the next one, someday, far away
Or maybe never, because it might be never.
That is a thought we don't have until

We're old enough to appreciate it.

Afterwards, I had more things planned,
But my father, at this rare opportunity
Of visiting family, seldom seen,
Asked me to find an old video tape -
An ancient and apparently much-played
Collection of vacations at the beaches
Of northwestern Michigan, years and years ago.

It was from a time when he was young,
Much younger than I am now,
Strong and hearty, at his humorous best,
Trading banter with my aunt and uncle,
And my late mother, as he flexed his still-young
Muscles and flashed a handsome smile.

We watched as he and my mother
Forged their way up sand dunes,
Or tossed food at the careening seagulls,
Or simply sat and silently sipped their coffee
On the sand at sunrise or sunset.

The colors were faded, and the sound track
Was largely washed-out except for the incessant
Repetition of waves crashing and receding.
It flickered and blurred to static in places,
But it still played, despite the years and the use.

I looked at him, sitting beside his walker,
Recovering from his latest hospital stay,
His hearing aids turned up to catch

The lilt of our laughter at his amusing antics.

The look in his eyes and the smile on his face
Spoke with a volume the video could not,
And warmed the room, for a time at least,
Against the outside chill, the incessant rain,
And the relentless approach of winter.

⌘ Bells

I have not heard church bells
In a long time. Years maybe,
Hospital bells? Yes. All too many.
Bells, beeps, buzzers, bleats,
All calling out for attention,
All warning that something,
Some small detail of life,
Like breathing or bleeding,
Has gone wrong somewhere.

Yes, life is in the details.
In the tenuous thread of care
And caregiving. A human thing.
The most human of all things
That should not be lost, somewhere,
In-between the grace notes
Of the song sung by machines.

II.   In the South

⌘ Propagating

I spent part of the day spreading seeds,
Something I never thought to do as a child,
Unless you count blowing dandelions.
Growing up in midwestern America,
When nature was always a given,
And not yet imagined as a thing with needs.
I decided, somewhere along the way,
That nature was due for some nurturing.

The seeds were Plains Coreopsis,
And their scattered husks, newly
Harvested, will ensure the return
Of bright yellow flowers with brown centers,
Blooming long and prolifically, popular
With small lizards and even smaller insects.

My home does not look like its neighbors.
Yes, there are a few palm trees and the colorful
Landscaping plants favored by Florida realtors

In the 60's and 70's, and still prevalent today,
But they are a minority, inherited from
The prior owner, planted decades ago,
And of no interest to wildlife.

Over time, one hurricane after another
Stripped away much of the tree cover,
Opening up the sky to sun and rain,
And providing me with a new canvas
On which to reinvent my surroundings.
To create an open invitation to life.

Where once there was a monoculture lawn,
Flowering trees and shrubs now billow up,
And a dozen beds spill wildflowers
And our favorite weeds in all directions,
Powerful attractors for things that fly,
And hop, and crawl, and ooze, and slither.

My neighbors shake their heads
At the tumbling milkweed,
The beggar's tick and dog's bane,
The frogfruit and water hyssop,
The richardia and the coonties,
The carnivorous passion flowers,
The sensitiva and the green shrimp plants,
And the mounds of narrow-leaved plantains.

Things that grew here long before
The conquistadores ever ventured forth
To infest the New World with their
Diseases, their ambition, and their greed.

Before the Puritans fled prosecution
To find a new home where they
Could themselves become the prosecutors.

Things that thrived here long before the
Creek and Yuchi and Seminoles
Fought the invading armies
To a standstill in their last stronghold,
Land so inhospitable that no settlers
Wanted to steal it from them,
Until the Army Corps of Engineers
Sliced through it with canals and levees
And drained it to plant orange groves and
Build tracts of identical retirement houses.

But where so many homes are urban deserts
Filled with pointless, purposeless foliage,
Mine is a year-round banquet
For all manner of living things that revel
In the abundant nectar and pollen and wealth
Of host plants on which to reproduce.
For things that belong here, and should be here,
Who have as much, or more right
To this place than we do.

I cannot change the past, I can only
Do my best to ensure a stable future
For a small fraction of the things
That should be here - the butterflies, skippers,
Dragonflies, and swarms of bees,
The woodpeckers and white ibis,
The ducks, and the grackles,

And the lizards of course.

I once tried to compile a list
Of all the different things growing in our yard.
I gave up after a hundred lines,
Realizing that counting or enumerating
Was unimportant. Life does not need
To be tallied on so small a scale.

Instead, I fill the role of arbiter, ensuring that,
In our limited space, the sweet-potato vine
Does not choke out the culantro,
And the ambitious grape vine
Does not kill off the Dutchman's Pipe,
And the alfalfa gets along with the partridge peas,
And the Spanish Needles -
The most prolific of all things -
Do not take over the universe.

⌘ More Than a Little (RoD)

Karim Kamel was an airship pilot
Who had spent the last seven years
Flying across the African continent.

He was born outside New Dakkar,
Seventh among nine children,
Closest to his younger sisters.

He liked his family, and visited often,

But they did not really need him,
So he chose a life of adventure.

Growing up, he read of aeronauts
From the golden age of flight. He wanted
To be a pilot. More than a little.

He trained and worked in Gaborone,
Flying above game reserves, counting
Abundant wildlife, scarce elsewhere.

He had a knack for flying. Soon
He was piloting medical supplies
And doctors from Cape Town,

To Kinshasa, and Dar-el-Salam.
Sunrises, sunsets, vast silences,
He felt fully one with the sky.

And then, he met a man in Harare,
An American, seeking trained pilots.
He was persuasive, more than a little.

"You are good Karim. Would you like to earn
More money? See more of the world?"
"How much more, and how much more?"

"All of Africa, from the Libyan coastline
To Cape Town, from Djibouti to New Dakkar.
Mountains and deserts, jungles, forests, plains."
"And the pay? More than a little?"

"Much more. Double, maybe triple."
"And what must I do to earn so much?"
"Keep secrets secret, be discreet."

Now he was piloting fast, agile airships
That ranged across the whole continent,
Conveying a specialized cargo.

His passengers were spies - observers
Who kept watch on disruptor groups,
Staving off wars and insurrections.

It was fascinating, testing his skill
Time and again, delivering or retrieving
Agents from the midst of hostilities.

He flew in darkness, watching the feed
From infrared cameras, hovering silently,
And leaving stealthily, secretly.

He dropped agents into farm fields
Or onto city rooftops, or snatched them
From treetops. Once from careening camelback.

Before long he had invested his earnings
In over a thousand goats, tended by
His younger sisters back in Senegal.

"Why goats?" the American asked.
"Goats are the safest of investments.
They can survive on almost nothing.

And they can make more goats,
And if anything does happen to them,
At least there will be meat in the stew."

And then he met a woman in New Dakkar,
With flashing eyes and graceful curves.
She was a university student.

He was smart enough to recognize
She was far smarter than he, but still,
She liked him. More than a little.

She graduated while he was away,
Flying alone across the Libyan desert.
"I am sorry I was not there with you."

"No matter. There is somewhere else
That I want you to be." He smiled.
"Back in New Dakkar with you?"

She shook her head. "I am leaving.
I want you to come with me. Mid-Ocean Six,
One of the great floating islands."

"That is the other side of the world."
"Yes. But we will have each other.
 "And the pay? More than a little?"

"Enough for a good life together.
Gift your goats to your sisters.
They will love you even more."

He was thoughtful for a while.
"And you, do you love me?
And must I learn how to swim?"

She laughed and smiled at him.
"Yes, Karim, that is a good idea.
And yes Karim, more than a little."

⌘ Self Portrait as a Spare Bedroom Office

(from a February 2022 writing workshop by Kai Coggin)

I am what surrounds me,
The books I've read, and the books I've written,
Photos of family and friends
Spanning a century. A little dated now.

My then-young children are adults.
My spouse, who ages so agelessly.
And other faces, many forever gone.

A jumble of electronic gizmos,
My tether, my leash, and my
Window on the wilder world:
My camera, and its myriad lenses.

Drawers filled with tchotchkes and mementos.
Keys to things I no longer own.
Dried-up pens, hardened erasers.

Eye loupes for seeing the small things
That have become fuzzier with time.
Things to be filed. Things to be shredded.
Things I cannot make up my mind about.

The desk itself, a rickety thing bought
Years ago for an aforementioned child,
Rebuilt with salvaged wood and made
Indefinitely serviceable once again.

A guest bed, little used in pandemic.
A list of things to be explored: new jobs,
New music, new poets, new places.
A list of fractal transforms to delve
Into, revealing concealed worlds.
Cups full of seeds from the garden,
Wildflowers to be propagated,
Casting their fate to the winds,
And maybe my own, yet again.

A familiar chaos, well worn
But still mutable, evolving
With time, need, and opportunity.
I am what surrounds me.

⌘ Nine Ways of Responding to a Robocall

Homage and apologies to Wallace Stevens

i.

Greetings Car Warrantyman. Pay me no mind.
My vehicle is much younger than I. I will roll the dice,
And see which of us expires first.

ii.

Dear Windows Server Person, I am sorry my machine
Is causing errors on your Network. Funny,
I don't remember having one. What would it look like?

iii.

Dear boy who is not my grandson, bail yourself out,
My own flesh and blood never made it home
From foreign wars. Death grants no reprieve.

iv.

Dear girl who is not my daughter after a car accident,
Next time, call someone whose name is easier to
pronounce.
Your nose is not broken. It should be.

v.

Dear Social Security Senior Service Center,
One of us knows I am not yet eligible for payout.
You will have to be a very patient thief.

vi.

No, Insurance Lady, I am not planning
On having any Final Expenses. There is a spot
In the vegetable garden with my name on it.

vii.

No, honey, I don't want a reverse mortgage,
I will be donating my house as a nature sanctuary
To local birds, bees, bugs, and weeds.

viii.

Dear dilapidated sports star of the last century,
I'm sorry that your ego outlived your self-respect
By such a wide margin. Greed is unbecoming.

ix.

Dear supposed billionaire pleading desperately
For my five-dollar donation. Really? You need it
More than I do? Have you no shame at all?

⌘ Walking in the Woods

I went walking in the woods today,
For the first time in a very long time.
I have walked among trees, but not
On wooded ridges and ravines
Peopled with oak, maple, poplar,
Sycamore, black walnut, beech and ash.
Not over ground thick with fall leaves falling,

And the wilting wisps of wildflowers
And skeletal fallen logs fletched
In soft green mosses
And finely fringed fungi.
Not while sleek fox squirrels skitter
Among the auburn aftermath
Paying heed to the hints overhead,
To the threatening tread
Of the twisting, gusting winds
Tossing the tasseled treetops
And hissing hauntingly through
The last lingering leaves.

I went walking in the woods today,
And remembered, for the first time
In a very long time, just what that
Sound sounds like, and how much
I like hearing it, and have long missed it,
Missed the sense of wonder and
The sense of adventure and
The sense of mystery it has always
Created for me, as if contained
Within it were warning words
Concealing captured wisdom,
Whispered in a long-lost language.

I went walking in the woods today,
And felt the yielding loam cushion
My measured footsteps,
And remembered, for the first time
In a very long time, just what that
Feels like. To set aside cement and

Asphaltum and tile and linoleum,
And let my soles scamper across
Something soft, supple, almost alive
In how it remembers my footprints.

I went walking in the woods today,
And remembered, for the first time
In a very long time, how the fall light
Lacks the intensity and insistence
Of its summer cousin, and how,
As its chiaroscuro contours are
Filtered by the flittering layers of life
Above me, its soft shadows descend
And dance delicately on the leaves
And the dirt and the moss and the
Bouncing, burbling streams.

I went walking in the woods today,
And realized that there is no substitute
For the incredible complexity
Of its sensory reality. No better way
To appreciate and admire
The evident truth of summer's
Passage into fall, and admit
That fall will be followed by winter
Soon enough. Dates on a calendar
Lack any vestige of these sensations.

I went walking in the woods today,
And conceded that spring and fall
On wooded ridges and ravines
Are the truest measure of time's

Persistent passage,
And yet, I also know that
The repeating rituals of nature
As the seasons change, are the
Earth's most genuine gesture,
To teach, and remind, and reassure us,
That time will indeed continue,
That after every winter, after every storm,
There will be rebirth, and renewal,
And yes, eventual decay, but then,
Everything will begin again.

⌘ Kaili (RoD)

The King of Dreams sat perfectly still,
Feeling the welcome warmth
Of the morning sun on his pallid skin.
He sensed he was not alone
And opened his eyes, focusing them
On the small shape before him.
A young girl, perhaps seven or eight.
A refugee – one of the newcomers.

"Hello, little one. What is your name?"
She stared at him in silence.
As he looked more closely, he observed
Her thin, malnourished muscles and
Swollen joints. She was trembling, and yet
She stood her ground despite her fear.

He asked again, kindly, softly,
"Hello, little one. What is your name?"
After some hesitation, "Kaili."
A faint, feathery voice. He nodded.
"A beautiful name. It means Destiny.
Do you have a question for me?"

"Are you . . . really . . . a ghost?"
"No. Not really. That is what they call me
Because of how I look. Have you known
Anyone else who looks like me?"

She nodded slowly, her throat tightening.
"My . . . mother . . . after she died."
A shudder ran through her frail body.
"I didn't know how to tell when
She was dead. She was sick for so long.
And then she wouldn't eat . . .
And then she wouldn't even drink . . .
It was harder to tell
When she stopped breathing."

He nodded in understanding.
"I am sorry for your mother.
Life is the cruelest of teachers,
Ever taking away what we love."

His skeletal fingers reached out
And gently, carefully, drew her closer
Until her head was nested against his chest.
"Listen . . . for the heartbeat. It is slow,
And it is faint, but it is there.

There was a time when everything
Was taken from me but that.

Yours is small, but strong, and steady,
And brave. Life has not given up on you.
Don't be afraid. Close your eyes.
You are safe here. Rest now. Dream.
I will keep Death away. I promise.
 I make few promises . . . but I keep them all."

As he held her in his arms
And rocked her to sleep,
He sang the soothing words
Of an ancient lullaby,
In a lost and forgotten language,
Then whispered to the Guardian Spirit.
"Who looks after this small creature?"
"No one, yet. She was a stowaway.
You are the first she has spoken with."

He stared at her sleeping face - and at
Her sunken eyes that were not unlike his own.
"Send me clothing, water, and food.
Something easy to begin with.
I will make sure she eats, then
I will take her to the doctor afterward,
And then to meet her teacher.
Find her a home, one with loving parents,
And an older sister to watch over her."

"Yes. And for now?"

                    "For now . . .

I will stay with her until she awakens.
There may be nothing more important
The King of Dreams will do
In this lifetime . . . or the next."
He looked at the girl. "Destiny." He whispered.

Whose destiny? The Guardian Spirit wondered.

From across the Common Room,
Aiata the cook had watched this encounter
And now watched as the King of Dreams
Stared off into space, lost in thought
While the small child slept soundly
In the safe harbor of his arms.
She looked at his thin, bone-like hands,
And pale, deeply-scarred face,
While a steaming pot of fish broth
Bubbled slowly on the fire behind her.

There is life and death in those hands,
She thought, remembering how she stood by,
Helpless, her own hands drenched in blood,
While a younger version of the King of Dreams
Worked with desperate speed
To save her niece's life, Oriata, the same niece
Who now stood beside her, expressionless,
Kneading bread for the mid-day meal.

⌘ Construence

It is not enough. It never is.
You are forever unprepared.
The battles you face in life
Will always exceed your
Inexpert estimations.
It's not your fault, really.
Life's challenges change
Cheatingly with time.

Childhood is bumps and bruises,
For the fortunate, full of
Sitcom sensibilities
Where all issues are resolved
In thirty minutes or less
Minus commercials,
Or, unresolved, become
Fodder for future fears.

Adolescence is a puzzling
Peppering of angst and
Adrenalin, urges, overthinking,
And binging on new sensations,
All abbreviated badly
By the boppity rhythms
Of a three-minute single
With miss-mouthed lyrics.

Adulthood is about aligning identity
And meeting a mate, a game
In which there are too many rules,

And strangely, at the same time,
No rules at all. Unwritten rules.
Dancing in the dark sans music.
Early success is a gift for some.
For others, a lifetime of looking.

Parenthood is the first true
Portion of pain, an exercise
In fretting and fear, in watching
And waiting as small copies
Of ourselves do things we know
Will lead to bad ends,
Imagining all the infinite ways
They will go awry. Then go awry again.

Parenting gives way to mentoring,
Giving hopeful hints to those
Questions you, yourself, have yet
To learn your own answers for.
Strange, isn't it? To hear your
Parents' trite homilies and
Words of warning leaping, unasked,
From your very own lips?

Next there is a period of coasting,
When bad things happen
To other people in other places.
You listen with confused empathy
To friends and co-workers
Telling vague, circuitous tales
Of episodes, and doctors, and
Rehabs, and therapists.

And then, unexpectedly,
You are thrust again into action,
Parenting your own parents,
Realizing how fortunate
You are to have them, and also
Realizing the pain and bewilderment
They live with daily, as nothing
Will ever again be what it should be.

And then, not unexpectedly,
It will be your turn one day,
And you will be the target of
The very things that they suffered with,
And realize, for the first time, the full measure
Of every ragged breath,
Of every stammering step,
Of every golden glimpse of sunrise.

My own advice, for what it is worth,
Is to saver and store away against
Future deficits, all of those fine, finite
Moments, weaving a filmy fabric,
A net to capture and indelibly
Imprint memories as ammunition
Against those battles you know
Are coming. Coming closer. Ever closer.

⌘ *Res Maneri*

As a student in secondary school,
Somewhere in the last century,
I studied the Latin language,
Like Greek, one of the roots
Of so many of the words
We use to describe the people
And places, and things in our lives,
And how we feel about them,
And how we categorize them,
And how we remember them.

I have the habit, since childhood,
Of placing things into unlabeled boxes,
Sometimes sorted, sometimes not.
Some are things that might be useful,
Someday, for something, a thing
I can't focus clearly on right now,
In the here and now that I am in.

Other things go into boxes clearly
Labeled with the Latin term *RES MANERI*,
An artifact of my teen years,
When I was enamored with
The secretive ins and outs
Of the language. It's hidden
Clarity. It's hovering on the edge
Of that which is known and namable,
And that which is lost and unknowable.

MANEO possesses one hundred

And twenty-six verb forms. The one
I am fondest of specifically is
The present passive infinitive form.
Thus the phrase implies that
These simple boxes contain things
That remain or endure or persist
In the present, and maybe in the future,
To maintain continuity
With pieces of the past.

But in passive form, more accurately,
The phrase implies things
Being retained, or endured, or remembered.
Kept safe against the rippling
Passage of time and thought.

Every few years I open a box
And look at what's inside, a game
Of memory that transcends
Space and time. Sometimes
There is an object found that
I can no longer correlate,
No longer attach to a memory
Of a person, or a place or a happening
That I wanted to remember,
To be transported back to.
Sometimes, but not often.

Mentalists speak of building
A memory palace, a place to house
Those things that you want
To be recallable, against all odds.

My palace, my Latin taxonomy of thought,
Lives in a row of random boxes
Across a closet shelf, filled with
Small objects and photos and paper scraps
That are meaningless to anyone but me.
But as long as I exist, so do they.

Those memories, and the people
In them, still endure and persist, in a way,
Even though they may be long gone
From the face of this earth.
In that sense, they are still there,
Among the *RES MANERI,*
The things that remain,
The things to be remembered.

⌘ History's Shadow

Our past is always with us.
Unseen, unheard, it follows us,
Steering our conscious thoughts and actions
In ways we cannot perceive,
Guiding us, warning us, comforting us.
It is a companion that will not desert us,
Not in the brightest glare of day,
Or the darkest cold of night.

We remember only
What we can remember,
But forgotten words and deeds,

Feelings and fears and fallacies,
Actions and inactions,
Pull for and against us,
Drawing us into the same trap
Time and time again,
Or leading us away
Through signs and signals unseen,
To the right place, at the right time,
To meet the right person,
To do the right thing,
To avoid temptation,
To be delivered from evil,
To survive, to live, and to thrive.

If you disagree with this view,
If you are one of the very few
Who understand who you are,
And why you do what you do,
Good fortune to you.

But know also, that you did not,
Imagine yourself into being.
Your genes were not self-conceived,
And yet somehow, against odds
You cannot comprehend,
Between the pulling tides of
Chaos and calculation,
You came into being,
And still exist. Such a simple
Thing to say, but not really so simple,
A thing to do, is it?

No one knows all of the
Whys and wherefores
Behind the things that they do.
Be grateful if you understand some,
But be mindful that
Your past is always with you,
Guiding the rest.

⌘ Bearing Fruit

I watch my grape vine grow in fits and starts,
The long slender tendrils, the bright green
Of its first shoots each season, and then
The broad, ribbed leaves as it waxes
To its maximum extent for the year,
And blooms in tiny florets, almost hidden
Among its leaves on a trellis shared
With passion vine, and pea vine, and pipe vine.

Our plentiful bees will pollinate them,
And over time their fruit will grow slowly,
Eventually going through their own
Transition of form and color, From pale green,
To pinkish-green, to reddish-purple, and then
Finally, a dark purple misted with the haze
Of sugars, indicating that they are now
Ripe, and sweet, and good for eating.

The leaves will go through a second,
Late-season transition, as chlorophyll recedes

And hues of yellow, and red, and brown
Take over, and then it will just be the memory
Of the taste and texture in our mouths,
And the rough, brown texture
Of the vines themselves as they sit dormant,
Waiting for their genetic clocks to spark
Them into growth once again.

This particular vine is small but bore fruit
After only two years. Amazing to me,
After the years I have spent patiently
Waiting for my avocado and rose apple
To give us something more than shade,
Something more than the pleasure of
Watching them grow and spread
And fill their spot in the world with color
And motion and a sense of future
Possibilities - of scents and flavors and
Textures that will come, one day,
If we, too, can be patient.

What is true for plants is true for people,
And I know that may sound trite,
But I think that it is true, no matter
How much they exasperate me at times.
I know that if I am careful and plant
Just the right sparks in my friends,
And family, and especially my children,
It is possible, not guaranteed, but possible,
That I will live to see those sparks grow
Into things I can recognize, and enjoy,
And admire. And if I see no growth

Over time, If I fear these sparks
Have not taken root. I can,
Like any good gardener, wait
For the next season, the next opportunity,
And sow sparks once again.

III.   In the East

⌘ Keeper of Legends (RoD)

Uira stood at the rail of a listing derelict,
Listing herself, after a long life of sorrow
And pain few others could imagine.
Burned, beaten, abused, starved, parched,
Storm-tossed, alone. That she still existed
Was more than miraculous.

She bore the scars of her experience
On her face, her hands, and hidden beneath
Her clothing. Nearly toothless. Nearly hairless.
Her memory, despite her age, was largely
Intact. And her hearing. And her eyes.
Death had not caught up with her yet.

The derelict (the ship, not her) was abandoned
A century ago, limping here on dregs of petrol,
Anchored above a shallow lagoon.
Here in this graveyard of ships they called Home.
It may have been their home - no one knows -
Before the seas rose and made them homeless.

Before they were scattered as refuges, unwanted,
At a time when the world had bigger problems,
Before they found their way back, to here.
It was a meager life, on their archipelago of rust,
Their existence was ignored by the world,
But still, somehow, they persisted.

She looked down at the ragged children
At play on the rusting barge below,
And recognized them, every one.
Her eyes singled out the tallest figure,
Oriata, wind-wrapt in her dark hair,
Her amber eyes full of mystery,

And startling depth. "Perhaps," she thought,
A taller version of me, of what I once was,
In my own childhood, all those years ago."
Oriata, whose name meant 'she who
Dances on clouds,' glanced up
At the old woman. How old, no one knew.

Oriata wondered what Uira was thinking
As she gazed out over the ocean,
Lost somewhere in a lifetime of memories.
Viewed a certain way, she seemed edged in light,
As if captured within her was some small fragment
Of the lightning for which she was named.

At other times, she seemed edged in fire,
As if the fire god himself had tried to kill her, and failed,
But left his mark upon her more visibly than all the rest.

For all of us bear his mark in some way,
She acknowledged, turning toward the horizon
And trying to imagine what Uira saw, that she could not.

⌘ My Next Adventure

I am job hunting.
Between assignments.
A Free Agent.
Currently unattached
To any corporate body.
Though thankfully,
Still inhabiting my own.

I am taught to smile and say,
"I am in search of my next big adventure."
As if I were a child of six or seven,
Forging a hopeful path
Through the unexplored territory of my sandbox
Armed with a pointed stick,
Anticipating a sumptuous reward
In the form of imaginary gold or diamonds
Or a magic talisman, proof against all evils.

But, in reality, it is what I am:
An adventurer, cautiously wading
Through the densely thicketed
Wastes of the online job boards,
Following the little arrow of my mouse
As I scout far and near,

Hunting for the rarest of quarries:
An opening with reasonably good pay and benefits
In some location that is not
Furnace Creek or Oskaloosa
And does not require a unicorn.

Who knew unicorns were so common now?
At least, that is what employers say they want.
They don't say it like that exactly.
They ask for ten years of experience in software
That has existed for four. They want
Doctoral degrees and "hands-on" experience
(And magical powers of divination.)
They ask for fluency in English,
Spanish, Polish, Russian, and Urdu
(Mandarin, preferred, with a Shenzhen accent).
They want young but mature, energetic yet wise,
Totally independent team players,
Laser focused, but with good juggling skills.

They say Tell Me About a Time
When you moved Heaven and Earth
And someone actually noticed.
Or a time you saved a lost soul,
Who was underperforming
For the Greater Financial Good.
In two minutes, more or less. (Preferably less).
Make sure your narratives include
The seventeen golden words we are looking for
But won't tell you. In reality we don't care;
We're only playing Buzzword Bingo.
Just tell us, why are you so bitter?

Didn't you read the book about the cheese?

I'm not actually. Nor depressed. Nor angry.
Nor frightened. Nor alone. Nor confused.
Nor was I ever fixated on the cheese,
Though I have navigated many mazes.
But I am not what I used to be.
My viewpoint has changed.
I have learned to separate that which I want
From that which I was told I needed.

I have found surprising happiness
In things I never took time to notice.
Reconnected with old friends, made new ones,
Written books, learned languages,
Taught things that needed teaching,
Kept my family healthy through a pandemic.
Gained new perspectives on myself, the world,
And maybe the meaning of life.

So yes, perhaps I am ready
For My Next Big Adventure,
And like the child with the sandbox,
As I explore (not alone - there are others)
I wonder whether I will find it, or it will find me.
There is a strangely appealing novelty
In not knowing what is next,
To having a map, but not a destination.
Life is all about the journey, after all.

⌘ Collecting Sunsets

All of my life, I have collected things.
Some people create or invent them;
Some prance and pirouette;
Some, who once did things, now teach them;
Some perform great feats while
Others, judgmental, only critique them.

There are other collectors
Besides myself. Many others.
Some gather praise, narcissitically.
Others garner insults, festering.
Many crave wealth, greedily,
Others claim moments of undivided attention,
Or expressions of anger, or ignorance, or wit.

I have even heard of those who,
With painful repetition, collect spouses -
Something I could never have done,
For of all things I have ever collected,
I know that of her, there could only be one.

All of my life, I have collected things:
Coins of the realms, postage stamps,
Colored shells and serpent's teeth,
Places that I've yearned to see,
Passing fancies, fleeting glances,
Time, with friends and family.

That last one I'd have collected more
Had I known it would come so rarely.

For when your years are new, you see,
A day can seem ever so long.
How was I supposed to know
That life plays so unfairly?
And how was I supposed to know
That so many faces would come and go?

I'm collecting sunsets now. And sunrises.
They are different, every one,
And while they are as ephemeral
As anything you can imagine,
No matter what happens,
Before long there will be another, and another.
And unlike most things, there is no fee,
No price of admission, no special gear
Required or knowledge needed. You don't need
To 'be' anyone. You can be Anyone.

I myself have been fortunate,
The last two decades and change,
To have lived on the eastern edge
Of the Everglades. The horizon
Is infinitely far, and the sun slides slowly
From the sky each night, never in too much
Of a hurry to fail to put on a show.

There are other sunset collectors
Who join me there. Looking out into
The clear open depths of eternity,
And watching, along with me, as
The colors slide through the spectrum,
From angry yellow, orange and red,

To subtle mauve, violet, and indigo.

Perhaps it is not sunsets I am collecting,
But the colors themselves, in the purest form
Available to me. I will make it a point,
While my sight is still able, to collect
As many of them as I can, and while we're
On the subject, might I add, that you should too.

⌘ The Geometry of Our Monsters

I went for a long walk this evening;
Five miles through woods
And meadows and wetlands.
The trail was good. There were
Deer and rabbits, hawks, bees,
Red-wing blackbirds, and river otters.

Plenty to keep my eyes and ears
Entertained and melt away
The miles trod by my feet.
But the lasting image, strangely,
Was something else. A line of
Impossibly delicate-looking
Electrical towers a hundred feet tall,
With high-tension power lines
Strung in long curving arcs overhead,
To the next tower, and the next,
Seemingly to infinity and beyond.

As an engineer I admired their
Elegantly contrived structure,
Of triangles perched upon triangles,
Their hexapodal arms spread
Straight out from their sides, like the
Exercise in which the T'ai chi master has his
Student hold out two heavy buckets
Filled with water. "For how long?"
The student asks, beseechingly.
"For forever," the master replies.

But my thoughts were not of the
Lacework of the design, or the
Necessity of having power lines,
But oddly, a scene from an old
Japanese monster movie,
In which these towers and their
Power lines always stood in the way
Of the monster's advance on the
Japanese metropolis (poor Tokyo!)

And it made me wonder,
About the post-war years in Japan,
And the foreign occupation, and the
Transition from an old world to a new one
Filled with unknown dangers and
Technologies and systems
Beyond experience or understanding,
And the shadow of nuclear horrors,
And whether the towers and wires,
And the wall they created were a savior,
Or a curse. Did they view modernization

As a benevolent future, or was technology itself
A monster, scarring the landscape,
Forced upon them from without?

All I really remember, besides the names
Of my favorite monsters and the persistent
Question of why the destroyed buildings
Of Tokyo never had any furniture in them,
Was that any construct created by mankind,
Any wall, or weapon, or machination,
Can only, at best, delay the inevitable.
It was not the towers themselves
That were the metaphor of interest,
But the wires in-between. The arcs,
And the knowledge that all stories
Follow an arc of some kind,
And that arc, that curvature,
Will have an inevitable result.

The real monster in these stories
(The monster in all stories)
Is not the straightness of the heroine,
Or the crookedness of the villain,
But the simple inescapable
Geometry of the plot, which must do
What it must do, in order to be a story,
In order to have the pieces we deem
A story needs to have to be worth
The time to tell, and to see or hear.

In that sense, we should always know
That the shape, the basic geometry

Of our monsters is of our own making,
Just as the true demons, in any
Horror story, are our own fears.

⌘ We're Doing It Wrong

Somehow, we all got it wrong.
Mathematics, that is. All of these
Years, decades, centuries maybe,
Children have been taught
The wrong parts of mathematics,
And as an inevitable result,
Most of them hate it.
Don't understand it,
Disparage it. Forget it as soon
As they pass their last test in it,
Or fail their last test in it,
And give up. Maybe forever.
Blaming themselves, or
Blaming the teachers who were
Teaching what they were told
To teach, or the parents who
Were as clueless as themselves.

The truth is we are doing it wrong,
And maybe always have been.
We teach numbers as if they are
Utilitarian things, and show how
They are used to solve obscure problems
We may never encounter in real life.

But that is not what they are.

So sad, so tragic, when all of this time
We could have been teaching that
Mathematics is a secret language,
A language that describes beauty
In ways that spoken words cannot,
That describes the shape of everything,
Or the sound of everything,
From the path of a dancer's feet,
To the rhythm of a drummer's beat.
From the shape of the clouds in sky
To the pattern of raindrops in the street.

Mathematics is the fractal language
Behind all that we see, or do, or are.
It gives size and shape to magic.
Think how different things would be
If we showed a child the simple
Beauty of the fact that the imperfect
Angle of one molecule of water,
One single, simple number,
Is the reason we exist, that all life exists,
And mirrored small or large
It gives rise to snowflakes,
The refracted colors of the rainbow,
And the tastes on your tongue.

Mathematics is the relationship
Of all things to all things, and the
Relationship of all things to one thing.
It describes things both infinitely

Large and infinitely small.
Things we can all understand easily
And things no one can comprehend.

We should begin teaching
This secret language with a mystical
Sense of wonder, and awe,
And heartfelt imagination,
As if we are imparting
The greatest secrets of the universe,
To the next generation
Of Magicians.
Because, in a sense, we are.

⌘ Forgetting

I've only spent one fall in the Midwest
In the last twenty-five years.
To be here again is a novel experience,
Or not so much novel, as an opportunity
To remember things forgotten.
Things like the tall golden columns
Of sugar maples lining the street,
Or the depth of clear blue October skies,
Or the chirping of crickets in chorus
As I hike through the fields,
Or the floating white tufts of milkweed,
As I collect seeds and cast some,
With their arrays of silken threads,
On to the winds to find their fate

Somewhere, elsewhere in place and time.

The strange but oh-so-familiar
Sights, and sounds, and scents
Of my parents' home - not my home.
The house I grew up in is elsewhere,
Owned by some unknown family.
I miss it, despite all of its flaws.

The house where my own children
Were born is also elsewhere,
I miss it too, though they remember
Only a little of life there, idealized,
Perhaps, as childhood often is.
But it was a good house, home to
So many of my favorite memories.

And as I remember the loss of one parent,
And carefully tend to the needs of another,
I wonder what memories of time and place
My children, now adults, carry with them,
And which they will forget, along with the many
They must have forgotten already.

I know undeniably, despite my attempts
To hold everything and everyone
In memory that I never wanted to lose
In the physical world, I have been
Forgetting many myself. Not
Due to senility, not yet at least, but because
New memories are always being made,
Blocking the old from sight until

Something, some trigger, brings them
Back into the light.

The scent of food,
As I cook one of my mother's old recipes,
The sound of footsteps on the stairways,
Changing the seasonal decorations,
From summer to autumn - pumpkin-orange,
Added to the yellow leaves and crisp blue skies.

Where is this going? Forward, of course,
Life needs to always be moving forward,
But on a wending path that takes me
In and out of the past. It is sad, and wistful,
And joyful in turn, but I am good with that.
And hope that my children, as they forge ahead
In their lives, have the opportunity,
At least sometimes, to follow a similar route,
Focused on the future, but bringing
The best parts of the past
The meaningful parts, with them.

⌘ Autumnal

I walked at sunset in the woods today,
        Watching the deer and rabbits
And enjoying the first hints of fall foliage
        And late-blooming goldenrod.

I thought of seasonal poems by Millay,

And Dunbar, Helen Hunt Jackson,
And others, but Bierce is the one that stuck,
    A man of legendary wit.

The venue was Tadeusz Kosciuszko Park,
    On land once gifted to the General
For his role in the American Revolution,
    Land he probably never even saw.

Ambrose Bierce once wrote that
    "Freedom herself shrieked in pain
As Kosciusko fell; and on every wind
    That blows, I hear her yell."

Across the street, on a windy hillside
    Above the banks of the Scioto,
I watched a slow, multihued sunset
    Shading softly from violet to blood-red.

These lands were not really theirs for the
    Continental Congress to gift
To anyone. They were Wyandotte lands
    For centuries. Maybe since Adena times.

Beside me, on the bluff above the river
    Is a sculpted stone monument
To steadfast Leather Lips, murdered by tribal factions
    Favoring alliance with Tecumseh

Against the invaders, His body was cast down
    Into a hole in the earth, by legend,
A cave that still exists today. Perhaps his ghost

Mending Worlds

Still weeps and wails for the dead.

The monument beside me also watches the sunset.
        Its eyes have watched thousands from this spot,
Seen the western lands draped in sanguine hues
        Or tear-shrouded by autumn rains.

While some griefs lessen with time,
        This is the kind that only grows deeper,
And improves only in the sense
        That we understand it more,

The cruel treachery, and the backstabbing,
        The desperate struggles and the
Stinging defeats, the mystery of unravelling
        The lies of the invaders,

The promises of peace and free passage,
        Written for all intents and purposes
In disappearing ink. Leatherlips, I think, knew this.
        I imagine an alternate history,

One in which Kosciusko took up the cause
        Of the Federation of Western Nations,
And led them against the invaders.
        An interesting but pointless speculation.

The tribal nations lost a bloody battle
        At Fallen Timbers, a site to the north
I used to cycle past as a child, unaware
        Of the sadness buried there,

And unaware that this one event began
          An avalanche of westward expansion
For the invading Europeans, and many
          Trails of tears for the original Americans.

⌘ Dead Man Walking

I see my dead father daily, or almost daily.
His face in my social media feeds,
His photos on the wall of our home,
And his clothing, walking around our house,
Sitting at the dinner table, making breakfast,
Watching Netflix on the living room TV.

He's gone, of course,
But the week before Christmas,
My family flew in for the funeral,
And my youngest son (in his mid 20s)
Since retro fashion is always in,
Since everything old is always
New again, to someone, decided
That his grandfather's wardrobe
Was a goldmine. He asked to
Take some clothing home,
In remembrance of his grandpa.
What a nice idea, I said, take all
That you want since you are
The only family member it will fit.
He filled his suitcase, and begged
A space allotment in his sister's,

And his mother's, and mine.
And now I am surrounded by
Clothing styles of the 60's and 70's
That all look hauntingly familiar,
But in a good way. A sometimes
Comforting way.

Is that . . .? My wife asks.
Yes, our son answers.
We all hope for our genes to
Survive us, whether we understand
That or not. Sometimes it is the
Jeans that survive us, and keep
Walking around above the ground.
Sometimes it is both.

⌘ Creatures of the Air

Twenty-plus years ago, when we moved
From the rolling green hills of Kentucky
To the watery flatlands of South Florida
Where the tallest point within an hour's drive
Is either the trash dump or
A triple-decker highway interchange,
I realized, too late, how much I missed
Kentucky's varied topography.
But I also realized, before long, that while
My new home on the eastern edge
Of the Everglades was flatter
Than any board ever envisioned by

A carpenter, it was far from empty.
It was filled, to a surprising degree,
With birds of many feathers.

My children watched the daily parade
Of ducks and ducklings through the yard,
And the crew of white ibis that also
Came through daily, poking the lawn
In search of insects and grubs.
And the parrots chattering in the trees,
Or flying overhead in flashing green flocks,
And the woodpeckers (not the smartest of birds)
Pecking loudly at their own reflections.
And the grackles, more percussive
Than any drummer I ever heard,
And the grebes whose fearful cries
Warn everyone of danger's approach,
And the herons and egrets stalking
Prey with perfect patience,
Swallowing things that violate
Miss Piggy's cardinal rule of never eating
Anything bigger than your head.

But my personal favorite of all these
Feathered creatures, is not the biggest,
Of most colorful, or most elegant flyer,
But the one best adapted to the place:
The Anhinga, or as the Seminoles
Call it, chen-te fuswa, the Snake Bird.
I have an appreciation that for birds,
The world is not flat. They exist in three dimensions,
Soaring and diving, perching and pouncing,

Creatures of the air for whom falling
Is a fear they have long mastered,
With an elegance that makes us
Terrestrials look, even at our best,
To be clumsy, cumbersome cowards.

And yet the snake-bird does all others
One better: It can delve beneath
The mirrored surface of the sky
And fly within the water,
Seeking out its prey and spearing fish
With its razor-sharp beak.
What a strange freedom it must be,
To be fully at home
Flying in air and in water,
Able to fish in places
Too deep for other birds.
What a wondrous gift for nature to bestow.

But all gifts come with a price.
Anhingas have no oil in their feathers.
They cannot float. And they must sit
Patiently with wet wings held wide
To dry in the sun and wind
Until they can take to the sky
And be bird-like once again.

This makes them vulnerable
To predators. What strange
Feature of Karma insists on
Such compromises? Such
Limits to their otherwise

Amazing adaptation?
How is this fair? Or did Nature
Decide that unhindered,
Anhingas might take over
The avian world? And, like humans,
Disfigure the environment and
Send the world out of balance?
Koyaanisqatsi, as the Hopi would say?

Their handicap is readily apparent.
I wonder, what is ours? Or is ours
Not one, but a long list of things,
Many of them unknown,
And our true handicap,
Our true limitation,
Is the not knowing.

⌘ Mirror Man

I stand and face the mirror
Where my father brushed his teeth,
Brushed his short halo of hair,
Flossed, and did all of the other
Standard daily ablutions
Of an average adult for the past
Thirty-seven years and change
That he lived in this house.

Rising at dawn to start his day
And staring at the slow evolution

Of body and face,
Day, after year, after decade.
Repeating the process,
Almost verbatim, every evening.
He was thoughtful, humorous,
Adventurous (within reason)
Did his best to stay connected
And keep up with new friends and old
(He made them easily)
And did everything,
Daily ablutions included,
With an exacting precision
I always aspired to, though never achieved.

I look at the mirror and admire
The beauty of how it is situated.
A flat, flawless, reflective
Pane of silver, above a milky,
Alabaster-hued basin and counter-top
With matching silver faucet,
And two pendant lights
That illuminate the room, and the subject,
With perfect, shadowless clarity.
I miss that human clarity,
And the person who possessed it.
My eyes crawl over my own image,
Doing their own accounting,
Noting what is different, and what
Is the same, or at least eerily similar,
In the new face before it.

More than one author, or poet,

(Myself included), has ruminated
On the life of mirrors,
And what they see in us, as we look at them,
And what they would say, if they could.
I wonder if they miss the same reflections
That we do. The faces, the hands, the smile,
The sweep, or lack of hair.
The empathy, the resilience,
The sentience, the simple familiarity.
I take a razor and shave off my beard,
An artifact of nearly three decades,
And see a familiar jawline emerge.
Not mine. His. And realize
What the mirror already knows:
That all of the same pieces are there,
In some form, in some combination
Or permutation. In plain sight
Or hidden just beneath the surface,
And always will be.

IV.   In the West

⌘ Ruby Beach at Dusk

When you come to the edge of the world,
You will know it. It is like nowhere else.
The edge of your world may not be
The same as the edge of mine,
But you will know it when you find it.

Mine is a cool misty overcast dusk
On a beach of dark sand, scattered
With perfectly smooth granite pebbles
And splintered logs and clumps of bare roots
And small rivulets that run reluctantly
Down brush-clad, rock-strewn hillsides
Seeking to merge themselves with the sea,
Here, where all things come to an end.

Mine is a place where dark sea,
And dark sand, and darkening sky
Blend into a nebulous coexistence.
A thing with no contrasts,

A thing you cannot grasp
Between your hands, or photograph,
Or describe in a word, or sentence,
Or three-page-long-paragraph.

A place where contorted driftwood fragments
Sit lonely on the dark sands,
Posed by the shallow retreat
Of waters you hear more than see.
Where shattered white crabs
Lay prone upon the softly glistening
Dark sands, their decapodal limbs
Splayed out in display for no one.

A place where silent footsteps disappear
As the dark sands are smoothed
By the rippled water's edge,
As it advances and retreats
In slow, steady, rhythmic stealth.

A place where time has no meaning,
Except for the gradual fading
Of late summer light from
The dim western sky. Sunset
Is a theoretical thing, unseen, unheard,
Unrecordable, unmeasurable.

A place where widely spaced fires
Flicker like earthly stars
At intervals along the ridgeline,
Indicating the presence of humans,
Those unwilling to venture out

Towards the encroaching dusk,
Lest the dark sands swallow
Them, or what is inside of them,
Leaving nothing behind
But their crumbling outer shell.
That, for me, is the edge of the world.

⌘ The Curbstone - Revisited

After *The Child on the Curbstone* by Elinor Wylie

It never stops, it never ends.
You never cease to be a parent.
No matter how old they are
Or tall they get, or whether
They live a mile away
Or a continent away.
Once you have seen that small,
Squirming, squalling, helpless
Version of your other self,
Once they are as imprinted upon you
As you are upon them,
You too, are helpless,
Helpless to let go.

And yes, you are entitled
To take their joys as your joys,
To celebrate their existence
And all of their accomplishments,
That is a right you have earned.

But you have also earned
Something else. Something at
The opposite pole of the
Careening emotional sphere.
The place where worry and fear live,
The place where your imagination
Always makes a wayward turn,
Down the wrong dark alley,
Too near the cliff's edge,
Too far out to sea,
With the wrong crowd,
For the wrong reasons.

That place from which,
Scream all you wish,
They cannot hear
Your warnings and entreaties,
And you cannot
Unglue your leaden feet.
That too, you have earned.
And though it carries
No badge of merit,
No outward sign
Of the terrors
You are entitled
To bear for them,
Know that We know,
All those of us souls
Who have earned the same title.

And while that knowledge, of itself,
Cannot take way the pain of Knowing,

It may be that any sadness shared,
Is a sadness lessened, at least somewhat,
As your child steps off the curbstone
And ventures outward,
Into the whirling ebbs and flows of life,
Wading through the real dangers
You know about, and the far worse
Ones you can't find a way
To unimagine.

⌘ Homeless Encampment as NICU Ward

Two miles down the hill, at most,
From the Metropolitan Market,
A purveyor of pristine produce
And pricey proteins and
Gaudy, gluten-less goodies
Of all shapes, and colors,
And levels of decadence,

Two miles, maybe less, there
Lies a linear encampment,
Arrayed along a level reach
Of road, where those who live
Without water, or warmth,
Without salvation or sanitation,
Or gig-speed internet access,
Live out their allotted lives
In the polar opposite of decadence.
In wheel-less RV's, rusty vans

With painted-over windows,
In cars of forgotten eras
With spiderwebbed windshields
And newspaper upholstery,
In threadbare once-colorful tents
Now made monotonously monochrome
By time, and rain, and wind, and sun,
By car and bus fumes, and by the
Airborne detritus of the nearby steel mill.
They live behind tarpaulins,
Behind cardboard and moldy plywood
Held in place by rope and string and
Cinch straps and the ubiquitous
Crooked gray stripes of duct tape.
They live pressed up against
A chain-link fence, on muddy ground
And trampled parches of brown grass,
So out of place in an area
Where the hillsides are covered
In colorful, exorbitantly-priced homes
And the hills themselves sport
Every shade of green imaginable,
Lush with new life from spring rains.

On the other side of the fence,
Trucks and diesel engines rumble and
Railcars dump scrap steel in
Unannounced avalanches
At odd hours of the day and night,
Shift whistles blow shrilly
And buzzers bleat warnings
And furnaces belch heat and smoke

And glaring lights shine relentlessly
Throughout the raucous night,
Banishing stars and sleep,
Banishing any thought of peace,
Or privacy, or purpose, or sense of self.

It reminds me of the time
When our youngest child was born
With unexpected complications,
Such that his first weeks of life
Were in the neonatal ICU,
Surrounded by harsh lights
And startling sounds,
And strangers rushing
Blurrily past the small thing
In the plastic basinet.
Stared at, poked, prodded,
Naked and taped to tubes and
Tied to boards and starve-fed
In tiny dribbles by syringes
And probably wondering
Who he is, what he is,
Why he is being tormented,
And if this is all there is to life,
Or is there something more?

⌘ Why It Must Be What It Must Be (RoD)

The Artist stood alone before
The somber panel of judges,
Preparing to defend his vision
For the Tomb of the Martyrs.

"Tell us why, Nicolaides,
You have chosen this pose?
It is neither heroic, nor echoes
Any classical form we know.
It is like none of the other entries.
Besides the names inscribed
On the pediment, nothing about it
Says 'memorial' to us. In fact,
We believe it will clash
With every symbol, every aspect,
Of the Tomb of the Unknowns
That it would sit beside."

"You disparage my work
Because you cannot understand it?"

They conferred among themselves
And another panelist answered.
"We are not criticizing the quality
Of your work, Nicolaides. Indeed,
Your reputation is well known.
But yes, you are right, in honesty,
We do not understand it.
This pose, this expression,

As my colleague states,
This is not a memorial –
It is a provocation.
The woman's face is angry,
The flames she kneels in
Suggest she is in hell.
Why would our martyrs
Be in hell? The scars she bears
On her arms and her back –
There is no beauty in this.
What drives these choices?"

The Artist paced slowly
Past the jury, beginning calmly,
As if instructing a classroom
Of young students, but by the end
He was shouting.

"The goal of any piece of art
Is to convey a message,
For all art is a symbol,
And is made up of symbols,
And these are our tools of expression.
Purpose defines message.
What is our message here?
Upon what is this concept based?
You have answered yourselves
Without realizing it.
The purpose, ladies and gentlemen,
Is to fix a symbol in our minds
And in our hearts in such a way
That it can *never* be ignored,

Can *never* be forgotten.
That was Clio's intent –
The voice of history –
The mother of this revolution –
And this design echoes that intent
With a purity that my best works
Of the past cannot match.
Yes, her face is defiant!
Of course, it is provocative!
She is admonishing us that
We must never forget
The lessons of history!"
"Look at her! She is archetype
Of all of those martyred
For our freedom. She is scarred
From her battles – *of course!*
She has been beaten down
To her knees! The flames
Of agony rise around her – *and yet!*
And yet, she will never surrender!
She holds the arc of justice
As both a shield to ward off
Her oppressors and as a challenge
To future generations!"

He swung around and pointed
At each of them in turn.

"You must never forget –
And you must never forget –
And you must never forget!
That is what her letters say.

That is what the songs say.
That is what this piece says.
It is a warning – *a dark warning* –
To all of us – to never allow
The Wolves – or anyone like them,
To take control of this country again!"

He stopped, calmed himself down,
And continued in his teaching voice.

"And that, my friends, is why
This is like no other statue,
No other symbol, in this country.
It is also not a thing to be viewed
From a distance. It is a thing
To stand next to, and to touch.
To place your offerings before
The memories of those lost.
To run your hands over the base
And feel the power in the words,
And especially the names.
So many names. Clio challenged
All of us to protect this country,
And if we fail, you and I,
Then she, or someone like her,
Will rise up again, and hold us
Accountable for our failure.
That, precisely that, is why
The design for the Tomb
Must be this, and no other,
Why it must be what it must be."

⌘ Rainier

We all have places. Favorite places,
Favored because of who we were with
When we first saw them, or what
Time in our lives we associate them with,
Or the way they cause us to feel:
Proud, confident, inspired, serene,
Pensive, grounded, awe-inspired.

For me, one of those places
Is Paradise Valley, one mile aloft
On the middle slopes of Mt. Rainier.
It is often covered with snow
Until late summer, but when fall arrives,
It is filled with glistening evergreens above
Emerald grasses and fast-growing wildflowers,
Deer and woodchucks, Steller's Jays,
And the persistent sound
Of small cascades splashing down
Rocky mountainsides to merge into
The Paradise River, meandering
Its narrow way through
The center of the valley,
Before it travels farther south
And tumbles over Narada falls,
A sparkling cascade
Down a time-molded cliff face,
Casting its roar and its rainbows
Into the next valley below.
It is a living portrait of contrasts.

Briefly filled with the lushness of life,
Then entombed for three-quarters
Of every year beneath twenty
Or thirty feet of snow and ice.

The sunsets, over the shoulder
Of the mountain, range from
Gloriously florescent to
Sublimely opalescent.
Snowstorms at altitude
On a tall, lone mountain, facing the Pacific,
Are a dramatic enfoldment of cold,
And wet, and silence
And the constant realization
That one more step,
Just one, into the white, swirling
Winds, towards the hushed sounds
Of whispering evergreens
And invisible cascades,
Seeking out the edges
Of the hanging valley,
Might be a step into oblivion,
My skeleton entombed
Along with the valley
Until it reappears from beneath
The ice and snow in the fall.

A hard lesson, that one,
That such beauty and awe,
Such wonder and enormity,
Are not a place of safety.
It is a lesson I will remember. Always.

⌘ Van Gogh Would Poke Out His Eye

(In the manner of Bryan Franco)

There is a meme
Making the rounds lately,
A picture of a room,
A large room, filled with
Plastic sunflowers, covering
The floor, and mirrored
On the walls and ceiling.

And it bothers me
That so many people
Would celebrate
Yet one more use
Of distilled and dyed dinosaur goo
To make artificial faux beauty
In imagined celebration
Of a dead artist whose life
Was filled with real people,
Real places, and the feel
Of the wind on his face,
And the mud beneath his feet,
And his own blood dripping
Down his neck from his severed ear,
And somehow they see
No irony in this,
No betrayal of a man
Who spent a lifetime
Struggling to find a way

To describe his vision of reality,
To experience life at its most raw
And most genuine.

Rather than watch the
Bastardization
Of his life's work,
I think Van Gogh
Would poke out his eye,
And hang up his painter's smock,
And toss his brushes on the trash heap,
And sit in a corner, drinking absinthe
Paid for with borrowed francs,
And wonder what the dinosaurs
Would have to say
About all of this.

⌘ Hurricane Ridge

The first time, the winds were gale force,
And we felt frozen to the bone
Before we had walked ten steps
Away from the shelter of the car.

The second time, we rose in stillness
And silence, until we breached
The clouds' upper surface, and looked down
Upon an undulating sea of white cotton.

From atop the ridge, the many

White-capped purple folds
Of the Olympic Range comprised
The entirety of the horizon,

A realm of rock and ice
So massive and so majestic,
Such a thing unto itself,
That it creates its own weather.

A place where the trees
Can reach only so far, and the
Ground layer's limited life
Is a thin crust of lichens and moss.

A peninsula with crystal lakes
And tumbling waterfalls,
And salmon-filled cascades,
And a rain forest all its own.

The view from the ridge
Is the high-level view,
Only hinting at the wonders
In the valleys below.

But isn't that always how life is?
By the time you gain
Enough perspective to appreciate it,
You start to lose sight of things,

Lose sight of the myriad details,
That make up the pattern.
When we climb far enough

That we finally see the whole,
Our eyes, and our minds,
Can no longer identify the pieces.

⌘ Circus de Arte

Maintaining an art museum,
In this day and age,
Must be a continual exercise
In evolution for the curator.

A process of deciding
What artworks are still considered
Tasteful enough to display,
And what are now comprehended
To be too sadistic in their depictions
Of the suffering of the poor
For the amusement of the rich,
Of the debasement of women
For the salacious amusement of fortunate men.

Or perhaps, what historical
Narrative or justification
Can be delicately wound
Around a racially-charged painting
Depicting a child slave,
A slaughtered prisoner,
Or a captive odalisque.

Or what explanation

Can be given for the
Unconscionable vilification
Of dark-skinned peoples
To create devilish metaphors
So that the melanin-deprived,
Inbred gentry of Europe
Could feel joyously justified in their
Theft and subjugation of
Other people, other places, and other things.
In their God-given right
To be ungodly.

As I walked last week
Through the multi-hued halls
Of the Ringling Museum of Art,
I had this thought, as I browsed
The myriad artistic treasures
That John and Mabel Ringling,
Circus purveyors extraordinaire,
Were able to buy, for a song,
From the aforementioned European gentry,
At a time in history
When fortunes were changing,
And American wealth was rising
As European wealth was cratering.

The New World Robbers robbing
The Old World Robbers.
Not that the Americans were blameless.
Far from it. Ask any persecuted Native American
Or subjugated African American
Or abused immigrant worker in the

Sweatshop factories
Just across the river from
The New Colossus,
Or the entire female half
Of humanity that had
Essentially, no rights whatsoever.
Then, as now, liberty is not a given.
It is not a static state of affairs.
The artworks of past ages hanging
On the prettily-painted walls
Are a graphic reminder for you to
Be mindful that the rich and powerful
Of your own generation
Will bait, and switch, and steal away your
Birthright for bread and circuses
As they are always wont to do,
And sadly, as they are always so adept at doing.
Whether it happens all at once,
Or in little pieces, so unassuming
You will not miss it until it's gone.

⌘ Heaven in Pink and Green

Behind our tropical home
There is a special tree.
A Dombeya Wallichii.
And this particular tree
Is heaven, to a bee.
To many, many bees.
Its large green leaves

(Larger than my head)
Require constant care,
But never have I
Regretted planting it,
For every year, without fail,
When it is winter up north,
My Dombeya explodes
In thousands upon thousands
Of pendant clusters,
Each with dozens
Of small, fragrant,
Nectar-rich, pink blooms.
A visual feast for us,
And heaven for the bees.
I can stand among them
Swarming by the hundreds,
Buzzing about fervently,
And they will ignore me,
So intoxicated are they,
So intent are they,
On climbing inside
Every single blossom,
And carrying away
Its bounty of pollen and nectar.
Somewhere, I know,
Maybe several somewheres,
There are rich combs of honey,
Uncommonly sweet,
And generations
Of unborn bees, dreaming
Of heaven in pink and green.

⌘ Mending Worlds (RoD)

(In the voice of series poet Natalia Yeka)

A great poet once said succinctly
(As she said so well so many things)
That after great pain, a formal feeling comes -
A numbness, an apathy, a means by which
We build borders around the holes in our hearts
That we lack the tools to mend,
Ensuring that we do not collapse
Beneath the weight of our grief
(And simply cease to be).

It is, at times, an impossibility,
To imagine an event that brings
Us back to a place where life blooms
Again. To build a separate peace in which
Happiness returns, (even in fits and starts),
And sadness comes softly to its end.
(An impossibility, yes).

Yet come it will, I know with certainty,
Because the heart, ever needing strings
To latch onto again, like weedy shoots
Seeking a slender sliver of sunlight,
will always search and stretch and strive
Until somehow it finds, (in sum or in parts),
A way to mend itself, and move onward.
(For life, to exist, must move onward).

V.   More?

112

Online Resources

Thank you for reading.

My other books are all available through my Amazon Author page: at https://amazon.com/author/spanoudis

Additional information and some discussions are on the Goodreads page for Stephen Spanoudis, or via social media at

https://www.facebook.com/therepublicofdreams,

https://www.facebook.com/theotherpages, or

https://theotherpages.tumblr.com/

I have also curated an annual poetry essay series with the assistance of Nelson Miller, Kashiana Singh, Bob Blair, and Robin Martin Berard. The Tumbler blog archive is the best way to read it. The 2021 series is also available as a podcast on Spotify, iTunes and other outlets. Search my name to find them.

The cover art was generated using JWildfire software using

114

a fractal flame script (Phoenician Garden) authored by
Imago Fracta. cf.: "We're Doing It Wrong," on page 74.

-- Steve Spanoudis, Coral Springs, Florida